William Howard Taft

oward Taft

Kieran Doherty

AMERICA'S

27TH

PRESIDENT

Children's Press®
A Division of Scholastic Inc.
New York / Toronto / London / Auckland / Sydney
Mexico City / New Delhi / Hong Kong
Danbury, Connecticut

Library of Congress Cataloging-in-Publication Data

Doherty, Kieran.
    William Howard Taft / by Kieran Doherty.
       p. cm.—(Encyclopedia of presidents)
Includes bibliographical references and index.
 ISBN 0-516-22967-2
  1. Taft, William H. (William Howard), 1857–1930—Juvenile literature.
2. Presidents—United States—Biography—Juvenile literature. [1. Taft, William
H. (William Howard), 1857–1930. 2. Presidents.] I. Title. II. Encyclopedia of
presidents. Second series.
E762.D64 2004
973.91'2'092—dc22   2003027244

Contents

Chapter 1

A Prophecy ─────────────────

One evening in early 1908, Secretary of War William Howard Taft and his wife were guests of President Theodore Roosevelt and his wife at the White House. Taft and Roosevelt had become close friends during their years of service together. Late that evening, President Roosevelt leaned back in his chair. After staring at Taft, he closed his eyes and pretended to foresee the future.

He said, "I am the seventh son of a seventh daughter, and I have *clairvoyant powers*. I see a man standing before me weighing about 350 pounds. There is something hanging over his head. . . . At one time it looks like the presidency—then again it looks like the chief justiceship."

Nellie Taft responded first. "Make it the presidency!" she said.

William Howard Taft replied, "Make it chief justice!"

President Theodore Roosevelt (left) with William Howard Taft. Roosevelt helped Taft get elected president in 1908.

The Roosevelts and the Tafts laughed together. Nellie Taft had long been ambitious for her husband, urging him to take on responsibilities that might some-day lead to the presidency. Taft himself had long dreamed of a seat on the nation's highest court. Some of the happiest days of his career had been spent serving as a federal judge. More than once he had told Nellie, "Politics makes me sick."

Eventually, both Taft and his wife would realize their dreams. Taft would indeed be elected president, and Nellie would be first lady. Years later, Taft would close out his long career as Chief Justice of the United States, the presiding judge of the U.S. Supreme Court. He became the only person in history to serve both as chief executive and as chief judge.

Birth and Childhood

William Howard Taft was born in Cincinnati, Ohio, on September 15, 1857, to Alphonso and Louise Taft. His father was a well-respected lawyer and Ohio polit-ical leader who would serve as secretary of war and as attorney general under President Ulysses S. Grant. Later in his life, he served as ambassador to Austria-Hungary and Russia.

Alphonso Taft had been born in Townshend, Vermont, in 1810. In 1841, he married and moved west, settling in Cincinnati. In 1852, Alphonso's wife died. At 41 years old, he was a widower responsible for two young sons, Charles and

Alphonso Taft, William Howard's father, served in the cabinet of President Ulysses S. Grant and also as a U.S. diplomat in Europe.

Cincinnati

Founded in 1788 after the Northwest Territory was opened for settlement, Cincinnati, Ohio, soon became a major port on the Ohio River and an important commercial center at the edge of the frontier. William Henry Harrison, a military hero in the Indian wars and the War of 1812, settled near Cincinnati in 1814 and was elected president in 1840. (He died after serving for only a month.) Rutherford B. Hayes, who made his reputation as a Cincinnati lawyer, was elected president in 1876, when Will Taft was in college. Benjamin Harrison, William Henry Harrison's grandson, studied law in Cincinnati and was elected president in 1888, when Taft was a federal judge. When Taft was elected president in 1908, he was at least the fourth president with ties to the city.

☆★☆

Peter. Later that year, while visiting Massachusetts, Alphonso met Louisa Maria Torrey (she always called herself Louise). In 1853, Alphonso proposed to Louise, and in 1853, they were married.

Louise Torrey Taft wrote to her sister that she looked forward to having children. "I delight in large families," she wrote, "and if my health is spared to me I intend to make it the business of my life for the next few years." In February 1855, she gave birth to a baby boy, Samuel. Sadly, Samuel died about a year later. Then, on September 15, 1857, she gave birth to another son, christened William Howard. He was welcomed by two older half brothers. Charles was about 14 and

The Taft home in Cincinnati, where William Howard was born.

Peter was 12. Later William also would have two younger brothers, Henry and Horace, and a sister, Frances (Fanny).

William Howard, called Will or Willy as an child, grew up in a prosperous family in a large, two-story house on a hill overlooking Cincinnati. Alphonso Taft could afford to provide a comfortable upbringing for his four sons and his daughter and to send them to good schools. In return, he demanded that they develop their talents. Once, when Will's rank in class dropped from first or second down to fifth, his father was displeased. "Mediocrity will not do," he said.

Outside of school, Will enjoyed playing baseball, swimming in a canal not far from his home, and ice-skating in winter. When he was about 12, he attended a local dancing school where, by all accounts, he became an excellent dancer. Even later in his life, when his he weighed nearly 300 pounds (135 kilograms), he was light on his feet, able to lead a partner around the dance floor with ease and grace.

College Years

In 1874, just a week before his 17th birthday, Will Taft traveled from Cincinnati to New Haven, Connecticut, to enroll at Yale College, one of the leading colleges in the United States. Will proved to be an excellent student. One of his classmates later remembered that he "stood high" not because he was brilliant but because he was "a plodder." A picture of Taft taken in his junior year of college shows him to be a large, heavyset young man. His hair was light and slightly wavy. In the photo, he looks serious, like a young man who knows what he wants and how to get it. One of his classmates remembered years later that Taft soon became "the most

Taft's photograph in the Yale class yearbook of 1878.

admired and respected man not only in my class but in all Yale."

In one of his letters home, Will told his parents about his busy schedule. Each school day, he said, he rose at half past six, then worked and studied and recited in class, with just a few breaks, until "ten, sometimes till eleven." Unlike many of his classmates, Will neither smoked nor drank more than an occasional glass of beer. He seems not to have enjoyed much of a social life while at Yale. He was selected for membership in Skull and Bones, a fraternity that has included some of America's most famous men. He also played baseball for the Yale baseball team. (Years later, George H. W. Bush, the 41st president, also played baseball for Yale.)

All of Taft's hard work as a student at Yale paid off. On June 27, 1878, at the age of 20, he graduated second in his class of 132 students. His father must have been gratified and proud.

Following graduation, Taft returned to Cincinnati. There, in the summer of 1878, he began studying law in his father's office. That fall, he enrolled in the

Cincinnati Law School. For the next two years, Taft pursued a leisurely course of study. Class work took only about two hours each day. It was not particularly difficult for a Yale graduate.

Like most of his fellow students, Taft found a job to fill some of his free time. He took employment as a reporter on a local newspaper. This job enabled him to spend a lot of time in the city's courtrooms, watching the law in action. When not working or going to school, Taft enjoyed his hometown's social life. By 1879, Cincinnati was a city with 250,000 residents and a lively schedule of culture and entertainment. It boasted a music hall, several theaters, and an excellent library. Will Taft and his friends went to shows at the town's theaters and enjoyed the entertainment in local saloons.

Cincinnati Lawyer

After two years of study at the Cincinnati Law School, Taft felt he was ready to take the *bar examination*, the test that would qualify him to practice law. In May 1880, he traveled to Columbus, the state capital, and appeared before a panel of judges, who tested his knowledge. He passed the exam, and received his license to practice law a few months before his 23rd birthday.

By this time, Will's father had retired from law practice, so there was no job waiting with his father's firm. For the next few months, Will continued

Cincinnati was a growing city when Taft returned after college to practice law.

working as a newspaper reporter. Then in October 1880, he was offered a job as assistant prosecutor of Hamilton County, Ohio, which includes Cincinnati. He quickly accepted the job and was sworn into office on January 3, 1881.

His appointment as prosecutor marked the beginning of a long career of public service. For nearly 50 years, William Howard Taft devoted his energy and skills to serving local, state, and federal governments in a wide range of positions, including president of the United States.

Chapter 2

Finding the Right Place

As a prosecutor, Taft tried swindlers and petty thieves and a few murderers. While he did a good job, he seems not to have been very happy with the job. In March 1882, just over a year after taking the position, he resigned to accept a more important appointment. President Chester A. Arthur appointed him collector of internal revenue for the Cincinnati District. He was in charge of collecting taxes owed to the government by businesses in the region.

Taft soon found himself even more unhappy with his new position. The work was boring. Worse, President Arthur instructed the young collector to dismiss employees who were Democrats in order to make room for faithful Republicans. Reluctant to take part in the political practice of rewarding party members with jobs, Taft resigned after only a year.

Out of public office, Taft formed a law partnership with Major Harlan Lloyd, an older attorney who had earlier worked with Alphonso Taft. For the next two years, Taft worked as a lawyer in Cincinnati. During this brief period of private practice, he remained active in Republican politics. He also courted Helen Herron, a young woman he had known for about five years.

Helen Herron Taft

Helen Herron, known to everyone as Nellie, was nearly four years younger than Taft. Her father and Alphonso Taft had been friends. Her mother and Will's mother "exchanged visits," and her sister and Will's sister Fanny were schoolmates. Will and Nellie first met in 1879, when they were introduced at a bobsled party. She was 18 years old and he was 22.

Over the next few years they met frequently. Then in 1884, Will began attending a "salon" Nellie organized, a gathering where a group of friends met to discuss books, art, and other interesting subjects. Will was tall and handsome, with a pleasant, easygoing personality. Nellie was small, pretty, well read, and intelligent. She was also a bit unconventional. Outspoken and intense, she wasn't afraid to speak her mind and wasn't above smoking cigarettes and drinking beer with her friends.

Taft and Helen Herron were married in 1886. Mrs. Taft urged her husband to pursue a political career.

Nellie was impressed by Taft's intelligence and was fascinated by his interest in politics and government. About a year before she met him, she had visited the White House as a guest of President Rutherford B. Hayes. She was entranced by the excitement of Washington, and she liked the Executive Mansion. She saw in Taft a young man who could become a political leader and might even become president someday.

In May 1885, William Howard Taft asked Nellie to marry him and she agreed. They were married on June 19, 1886, in the Herron home in Cincinnati.

Judge Taft ————————————————

By the time he and Nellie married, Taft was a familiar figure in Ohio legal circles. He continued his private law practice and also served as assistant county solicitor (county attorney). Then in March 1887, Ohio governor Joseph Foraker appointed him to a judgeship to complete an unfinished term on the Ohio Superior Court. Foraker wrote that Taft had "a strong intellectual endowment, a keen, logical, analytical mind, and . . . all the essential foundations for a good judge."

Taft was pleased and proud, partly because his father had served years earlier as a superior court judge. Nellie was less happy. While she supported her husband in his career, she found the world of courts and judges much less exciting than the world of politics. She feared that Taft might spend the rest of his career hearing cases and writing decisions.

Taft soon learned that he loved being a judge. Fourteen months after his appointment, he ran for a full term on the court. He won handily, with 21,025 votes to his opponent's 14,844.

Solicitor General

In 1888, Republican Benjamin Harrison was elected president. Although he had spent most of his career in Indiana, he had grown up near Cincinnati and had studied law there. After Harrison took office in 1889, a vacancy opened on the U.S. Supreme Court. Surprisingly, young Will Taft was mentioned as a possibility even though he was only 32 years old and had served as a judge for less than three years. The appointment went to another judge with much more experience.

Still, Harrison was clearly aware of young Taft's brilliance. In early 1890, he offered to appoint Taft Solicitor General of the United States, the lawyer who represents the federal government's interests, often arguing the government's case before the U.S. Supreme Court. Taft regretted resigning his judgeship, but the offer was too good to pass up. He accepted the appointment and traveled to Washington, D.C., to start his new duties on February 4, 1890.

Taft became Solicitor General of the United States, the government's top lawyer, at the age of 33.

Taft soon wondered if he had made the right decision. In a letter to his father, he said he felt "entirely unfamiliar" with the federal law he would have to practice before the nation's highest court. Nellie Taft had fewer doubts. She had faith in her husband's abilities and was excited about living in Washington. She arrived two weeks after Taft, bringing their six-month-old son Robert with her. When asked what she thought of her husband's new appointment, she was typically outspoken. "I was very glad because it gave Mr. Taft an opportunity for exactly the kind of work I wished him to do," she said.

Taft served as solicitor general for only two years, but he proved to be worthy of the job. He successfully argued more than two dozen cases before the Supreme Court and gained wider recognition for his abilities. He also met men who would play major roles in his later career, including Theodore Roosevelt and Henry Cabot Lodge.

In 1891, Taft faced a family tragedy. Alphonso Taft was now more than 80 years old. He lived in California with his daughter Fanny and her family. In May, Alphonso became gravely ill. Taft made the long train journey to San Diego, where he found his father drifting in and out of consciousness. Alphonso Taft died on May 21, 1891. Shortly before his death, he looked up at Will, who was seated by his bed. "Will," he said, "I love you beyond expression." Will returned that love. He grieved for his father for many months.

Theodore Roosevelt was an energetic and outspoken Republican from New York serving on the U.S. Civil Service Commission. He was a year younger than Taft and had already gained fame as an author and reformer. He would later become a hero in the Spanish-American War. As vice president and later as president, Roosevelt would help promote Taft's career, and the two men became close friends. Henry Cabot Lodge, who was a few years older, would soon be elected to the U.S. Senate and serve there for more than 30 years. During Taft's presidency, Lodge was one of the most powerful Republican leaders in Congress.

Henry Cabot Lodge, one of Taft's early friends in Washington, served as a U.S. senator from Massachusetts from 1893 to 1924.

Circuit Court Judge

In 1892, Taft was on the move again. President Harrison offered him a federal judgeship on the Sixth Judicial Circuit of the Court of Appeals of the United States. The Sixth Circuit Court included parts of Ohio, Kentucky, Tennessee, and Michigan. The court sat (conducted its business) in Cincinnati, so Taft's promotion required a move back to Ohio. Still, a position on the Court of Appeals was the highest judicial position next to Supreme Court justice.

On March 21, 1892, he resigned his post as solicitor general to take the new position. Nellie was unhappy to leave Washington, with its excitement and the chance to mix with the people she called "the big-wigs." Taft, on the other hand, was overjoyed. "I love judges," he once said, "and I love courts." For nearly nine years, from 1892 until 1900, Taft served on the Court of Appeals. In those years, he and Nellie and their children, Robert, Helen (born in 1891), and Charles (born 1897) lived in Cincinnati in a house rented from friends.

Taft's Increasing Girth

Taft fought obesity—and mostly lost—during his entire life. He was always a big, heavyset man, weighing 240 pounds (108 kg) when he graduated from college. As he grew older, he developed a pattern of gaining weight when he was unhappy and slimming down when he was content. Even when he was "slim," he weighed nearly 250 pounds (113 kg), but during unhappy times his weight would soar well over 300 pounds (135 kg). A widely told joke in Washington said that Taft was the most polite man in the city because he once gave his seat on a streetcar to three women.

People made good-natured jokes about Taft's size, but most people at the time considered it appropriate for a successful middle-aged man to be nearly as big around the waist as he was tall. In fact, a thin person was more likely to be suspected of being unhealthy than a fat one.

☆★☆

Taft's duties as a circuit court judge required him to travel extensively to hold hearings and trials. During his travels, he and Nellie wrote often. In their letters they often expressed affection for each other. In one letter, Nellie called Taft her "dear darling, lovely, beautiful, sweet precious boy." Taft spoke of his love for Nellie and their children. Once, after they had a minor argument, he assured her of his devotion. "I am so glad that you don't flatter me and sit at my feet with honey," he wrote. "You are my dearest and best critic and are worth much to me in stirring me up to best endeavor."

During this period, the Taft family spent summer vacations in Murray Bay, a small village on the shores of the St. Lawrence River in Canada. Taft loved the family's rented cottage above the St. Lawrence, with its view of the river and nearby mountains. The people of the village made Taft feel at home. They called him *le petit juge* (the little judge), with a mix of respect and humor, and raised their hats when he passed as a sign of respect.

Labor Troubles

Taft's term on the court of appeals was one of the happiest periods of his life. In the cases that came before the court, he was able to satisfy his curiosity about a wide range of subjects and to develop his ability to apply federal laws to ever-changing circumstances. He seemed to enjoy even the difficult cases that were

Strikes in the 1890s often caused violence and destruction of property. As a federal judge, Taft helped decide cases involving disputes between labor and management.

sure to upset the losing side. During his time on the court, some of the most difficult cases involved disputes between company owners (management) and workers (labor).

In one case, railroad workers went on *strike* (refusing to work until their
demands were met) against a railway company. Other railroad companies, afraid
that their own workers might strike, refused to carry freight for the company
whose workers were already striking. That company asked the court for an
injunction (a court order) forcing the other railroads to carry its freight. Taft sided
with the railroad owners and granted the injunction.

The railroad union accused Taft of being against the workers because his
decision made it easier for the owners to continue in business without settling the
strike. Yet in other cases Taft ruled in favor of workers. In one of these cases, a
worker injured on the job sued his employer for damages. The employer argued
that the worker knew the job he was doing was dangerous, so he did not deserve
damages. Taft ruled in favor of the worker, writing that a worker did not give up
his right to collect damages by agreeing to do a dangerous job.

In 1896, William McKinley, yet another Ohio Republican, was elected
president. Now Taft had reason to hope he might receive an appointment to the
Supreme Court. Yet when he received a summons from President McKinley, it
was for a very different job.

Chapter 3

War

While Taft was serving as a circuit judge, events were happening outside the United States that would change his life forever. In 1898, a dispute between Spain and the United States over Spain's colony of Cuba rapidly brought on a war between the two countries. A group of militant Cubans began a campaign for independence from Spain. Spain took military action to put down the revolution and refused offers by the United States to help negotiate a settlement. Many citizens in the United States favored the freedom fighters in Cuba, and they began to clamor for a declaration of war to assure the island's freedom. A U.S. warship, the USS *Maine*, was sent to Havana, the Cuban capital, to protect American interests there.

In February 1898, the USS *Maine* was destroyed and sunk by a massive explosion, causing the death of more than 200 navy men and

Fast Facts

THE SPANISH-AMERICAN WAR

Who: The U.S. against Spain

When: April 1898 through August 1898

Why: Americans supported a revolution against Spanish rule in Cuba and were outraged by Spain's brutal actions against the freedom fighters; businessmen wanted protection of their property in Cuba; the destruction of the U.S. battleship *Maine* in Cuban waters in February (supposedly caused by Spain) helped bring a war declaration

Where: Naval battle at Manila Bay, the Philippines, May 1; invasion of Cuba, June; naval battle near Santiago de Cuba, July 3; capture of Puerto Rico, July

Outcome: The U.S. defeated Spanish land forces in Cuba and destroyed Spanish naval fleets at Manila and Santiago de Cuba; Treaty of Paris, December 1898, gave independence to Cuba, ceded Puerto Rico and Guam to the U.S., sold the Philippines to the U.S. for $20 million

officers. Newspapers claimed that the explosion had been caused by a Spanish torpedo or mine, and the pressure for war mounted. Only weeks later, President McKinley asked Congress for a declaration of war, and Congress passed the declaration on April 24.

On May 1, a U.S. Navy fleet destroyed a Spanish fleet in Manila Bay, near the capital of Spain's Philippine Islands, halfway around the world from Cuba. Taft's old friend Theodore Roosevelt resigned his position with the Navy Department in Washington to help organize a volunteer regiment to fight in Cuba. Late in June, the regiment landed in Cuba with other forces, and on July 1, it helped capture the San Juan Heights, outside of Santiago de Cuba. Roosevelt led one of the charges up the hill, and overnight he became a national hero. Days later, the U.S. Navy destroyed the Spanish fleet near Santiago, and later in July

Taft's old friend Theodore Roosevelt (left) and General Leonard Wood (right) organized the First U.S. Volunteer Cavalry, known as the "Rough Riders." It helped defeat Spanish troops at San Juan Hill in Cuba in 1898.

U.S. forces captured Puerto Rico, another Spanish possession. By early August, fighting had come to an end, and the United States was victorious.

In the treaty ending the war, Spain agreed to grant independence to Cuba (under U.S. supervision); *ceded* (gave up) Puerto Rico and the Pacific island of Guam to the United States; and sold the Philippine Islands to the United States for $20 million.

A Change of Direction ─────────────────

Taft continued his work on the court. He certainly read about the war and the treaty, but was not involved in U.S. actions. Then, late in January 1900, Taft received a telegram from the White House.

"What do you suppose that means?" he asked, showing the telegram to Nellie.

"I would like to see you in Washington on important business," the telegram said. It was signed by President William McKinley.

The Tafts had no idea what the president wanted, but Taft lost no time in responding to the president's summons. In Washington, McKinley surprised Taft by asking him to join the commission that would govern the Philippines. Taft wrote years later, "He might as well have told me that he wanted me to take a flying machine."

President William McKinley appointed Taft to the Philippine Commission. Taft later became the first civilian governor of the new U.S. possession.

Taking a job so far away and so different from being a judge would mark a huge change of direction for Taft. He knew little or nothing about the Philippines. Yet the president was offering him a chance to participate in setting up a wholly new government for a new United States possession. It was a huge challenge.

President McKinley, with help from Elihu Root, the secretary of war, gradually persuaded Taft to take the job. They told him he would be in the Philippines for only six months or a year, and the president promised not to forget him for a judicial appointment when he returned. Taft finally agreed to take the

The Philippine Islands

The Philippine Islands cover a huge territory on the western edge of the Pacific Ocean, south of China and north of Indonesia and Australia. They were first visited by Europeans in 1521, when Ferdinand Magellan sailed into Philippine waters on the voyage that would take his ships around the world. Spain conquered the huge island group in the 1560s and governed for more than 300 years. Many of the native Malay people, known as Filipinos, were converted to Christianity by Spanish priests and friars and adopted many Spanish customs and holidays.

The Philippines remained a possession of the United States from 1899 until 1946, when it became an independent nation, known today as the Republic of the Philippines.

☆ ★ ☆

job, provided he was made the president of the commission. McKinley agreed. The 43-year-old federal judge had taken on a major new assignment.

When Taft and his family arrived in the Philippines in the summer of 1900, the situation was grim. Philippine revolutionaries under the direction of Emilio Aguinaldo refused to accept government by the United States, demanding independence for Filipinos. Aguinaldo directed a bloody guerrilla war against U.S. forces. The islands had been placed under military rule and were governed by U.S. army general Arthur MacArthur. MacArthur lived in Malacanang Palace, the traditional home of the Spanish governors-general who ruled the islands before the war. The Taft family rented a cramped house.

Taft immediately set out to learn as much as possible about the land and its people. He began interviewing Filipinos and Americans to find out what needed to be done. Working ten and sometimes twelve hours a day, he soon came to his own conclusions about the people. "The population of the islands," he wrote in a letter to Elihu Root, "is made up of a vast mass of ignorant, superstitious people." The people, he added, "are lighthearted, musical and good tempered. They are also light-fingered and the greatest liars in the world."

These early impressions seem patronizing, but the longer Taft worked in the Philippines, the more fond he became of the Filipino people. He soon understood that they were proud and resented any suggestion that they were inferior.

Taft (at right in white suit) at a Filipino celebration during his term as governor of the Philippines.

He believed they were not ready for complete self-rule in 1900, but he wanted to give the roughly 7 million people of the island chain as much control of their own lives as possible. The Americans, he said, were not entitled to do anything that did not have the benefit of the Filipinos "as its chief purpose."

General MacArthur had a much lower view of the Filipinos. He believed that they were simply incapable of governing themselves and were beneath any consideration. Taft rejected MacArthur's view. He entertained Filipinos at official and unofficial dinners and receptions. He traveled extensively. He was careful, too, not to say anything against the freedom fighters who waged war to drive America from the islands. For the respect he showed, he gained the respect of many Filipinos.

Taft's task was not easy. He sought to gain the trust of those who had welcomed American rule, yet at the same time he worked to persuade the rebels to stop their brutal conflict with the U.S. Army. His job was made more difficult in the fall of 1900 by a political leader at home. William Jennings Bryan, the Democratic candidate for president, was opposed to the American war and its efforts to form a government in the Philippines. Instead, he called for immediate and total independence for the Philippines. The call gave courage to the freedom fighters, and the war got worse.

In November, President McKinley defeated Bryan and was reelected to a second term. Not long afterward, the Filipino *insurrection* (uprising) came to an end.

The Friars

One of the thorniest problems Taft faced in the Philippines had to do with lands that had long been owned by the Roman Catholic Church. The church was one of the most powerful forces in the islands and gradually gained ownership of some 400,000 acres (160,000 hectares) of the best land. Much of this land was rented back to Filipino farmers at very high rates. As a consequence, the church friars had come to symbolize foreign greed and domination. Before the Spanish-American War, in 1896, Emilio Aguinaldo's army drove the friars from the Philippines and turned their rich lands over to the people.

Taft's problem was that the peace treaty ending the Spanish-American War committed the United States to protect the church's property rights in the Philippines. He was required by law to protect the friars' interests, but he wanted to find a way to keep the lands in the hands of the Filipino people.

Civil Governor

When the worst fighting ended in the spring of 1901, it was time for the U.S. Army to turn full control of the Philippines over to a civil government, to be headed by Taft. On July 4, 1901, at a ceremony in Manila, Taft was sworn in as the Philippines' first civil governor.

By that time, Taft was ill and tired. He caught a tropical fever that came and went without warning, and suffered from severe intestinal problems. Then, on September 14, 1901, President McKinley died after being shot by an assassin a week earlier. The Taft family decided to return to the United States so that Taft could recover his health and consult with the new government in Washington. They sailed on Christmas Eve.

In the election of 1900, Theodore Roosevelt had been elected vice president on the Republican ticket with President McKinley. When McKinley died, Roosevelt was sworn in to complete his term. When Taft reached Washington, he met with his old friend and with Secretary of War Elihu Root. He was pleased to learn that he had the full support of the government for his actions in the Philippines. He also consulted with Archbishop John Ireland, an influential representative of the Roman Catholic Church, about the problems with the friars' lands in the Philippines.

In the meantime, Taft had recovered his health and was eager to return to the Philippines. President Roosevelt urged him to visit Rome on his way, to discuss the problem of the Roman Catholic Church's lands in the Philippines. Taft arrived in Rome in May 1902. There he met with church officials, including Pope Leo XIII, the world leader of the Roman Catholic Church. Taft and the pope had a friendly meeting, but they were unable to reach a formal agreement. Taft was still negotiating a year later, when Pope Leo died. In November 1902, however, Pope Pius X, Leo's successor, agreed to sell nearly all the church's land to the Philippine Commission for $7,543,000. At the same time, the church agreed to reduce its influence in Philippine affairs. Taft's negotiations had

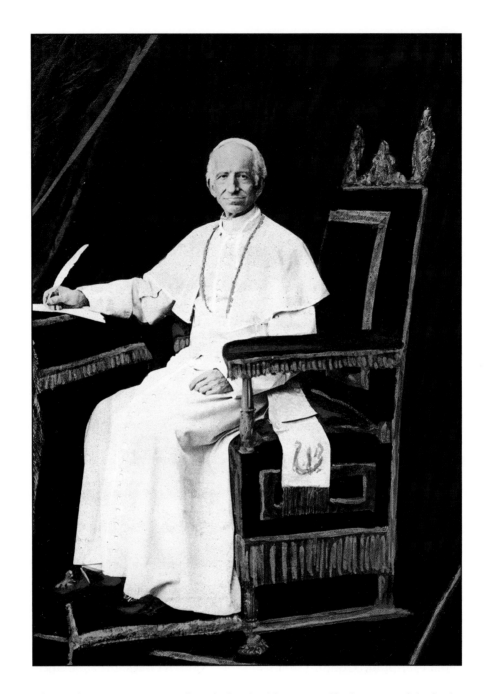

Taft met with Pope Leo XIII in 1902 to discuss lands in the Philippines owned by the Roman Catholic Church.

brought a resolution to one of his biggest problems. U.S. authorities sold the rich lands to Filipino farmers at low rates, giving them title to their farms.

A Time of Trouble

While negotiations continued with Rome, Taft arrived back in the Philippines in August 1902. The next two years were difficult both for him and for the Filipino people. First, the islands were ravaged by cholera, a deadly illness transmitted by contaminated drinking water. Eventually some 100,000 people died of the illness. In late 1902 and early 1903 the country was struck by famine. Then in June 1903 a great *typhoon* (a tropical storm similar to a hurricane) swept across part of the islands, destroying thousands of homes.

Even through all these trials, Taft worked methodically to put a government in place, establishing law-enforcement organizations and a series of courts to settle disputes and try those accused of crimes. He also worked toward a system in which Filipinos would elect representatives to one house of a legislature. Unlike General MacArthur, he believed that the Filipinos would one day govern themselves.

Taft continued to suffer ill health. His family, which had stayed in the United States, and his friend President Roosevelt worried about him. Once in 1902 and again in 1903, Roosevelt offered him an appointment to the Supreme

Laughing at Himself

In April 1903, Taft made a long trip to Baguio, a mountain resort about 120 miles (190 km) from Manila. The last 25 miles (40 km) of the journey were traveled on horseback under a baking sun. Knowing that Elihu Root was concerned about his health, Taft sent a telegram to the secretary of war. "Stood trip well," the telegram read. "Rode horseback twenty-five miles to five thousand feet elevation."

Imagining Taft on horseback, Root replied, "Referring to your telegram, . . . how is the horse?" When Taft read the answer, he roared with laughter. He later told the story to reporters and did not mind when the story was published.

In spite of his weight, Taft enjoyed horseback riding.

☆ ★ ☆

Court. Both times, Taft said he did not want to desert the people of the Philippines. Finally, on March 27, 1903, Taft received a letter from the president urging him to return to Washington. Once again, Taft would be asked to change direction. The president did not want him to become a Supreme Court justice. Instead, he wanted to appoint Taft secretary of war in place of Elihu Root, who was resigning.

At first, Taft did not want the job. He was still concerned about the people of the Philippines, and he knew that there was still much work to do. He was also worried that he and his family would not be able to live comfortably on the $8,000-a-year salary he would receive as secretary of war. He finally agreed to accept the post, however. In late 1903, he announced he would resign as civil governor of the Philippines to take on his new responsibilities in Washington.

Taft returned to the United States to a warm welcome. He had proved his abilities in a new and difficult area, helping start the Philippines on a journey toward self-government. Before he died, the United States had granted Filipinos substantial responsibility for governing themselves and was beginning to plan for the eventual independence of the islands.

Chapter 4

Adviser to the President ───────────

Taft soon became an especially close and friendly adviser to President Roosevelt. The president was just planning a campaign for re-election in the fall of 1904, and he was pleased to have his old friend close at hand to help manage the government. Roosevelt was a brilliant campaigner, popular with a large part of the country. He also performed brilliantly as president, seeming to enjoy every minute of his day and every responsibility. He had taken controversial actions at home and overseas, yet he still had broad support in his party and in the country.

Taft brought some welcome skills to Roosevelt's administration. The president had more ideas than he was able to put into action. Once a program or policy had been put into place, he tended to jump to another area of concern. He was impatient with details, and didn't have the concentration to work out complicated plans. Taft proved

Secretary of War

Taft's position as secretary of war put him in charge of the War Department, which had responsibility for the U.S. Army. The navy was overseen by the Department of the Navy, with its own secretary. Both secretaries were members of the president's cabinet. In 1947 the two departments were combined into the Department of Defense, which became responsible for all the military services. Today the secretary of defense is the member of the president's cabinet directly responsible for military affairs.

☆ ★ ☆

himself a master of careful planning, and he could help implement Roosevelt's ideas. In addition, where Roosevelt was outspoken and opinionated, Taft spoke quietly and sought to resolve problems by negotiation and diplomacy. In many ways they made a perfect match.

Upon starting his new job as secretary of war, Taft discovered that much of his time was spent attending cabinet meetings where the main topic of conversation was politics. This was a topic Taft found tiresome. Still, he was pleased to be in the cabinet and soon established a close working relationship with Roosevelt. "The President seems to take much comfort that I am in his cabinet. . . . I am growing to be very fond of him," he said.

Back in Washington, Secretary of War Taft poses in an impressive fur-lined coat.

Through early 1904, Nellie remained in California with their children, who were finishing their school year. Robert was now 14, Helen was 12, and Charles was 6. In May, they moved to Washington, and the family was reunited. They moved into a large rented house not far from the White House. Taft's financial worries had been eased by his half brother Charles, a wealthy and influential businessman in Cincinnati, who helped pay the family's expenses in Washington.

Nellie had loved being the "first lady" of the Philippines, but she was happy to return to Washington. She was also relieved that her husband had not been appointed to the Supreme Court. She still dreamed of living in the White House and believed that Taft's cabinet position might lead to the presidency.

Panamanian Troubleshooter

Taft soon proved his worth to the president as a problem solver. One of his first tasks was to help manage Roosevelt's pet project, the construction of the Panama Canal. In 1904, the United States took possession of the Canal Zone, a strip of land across Panama where the canal would be built to connect the Atlantic and Pacific Oceans. Engineers were at work designing the immense canal, but construction had not yet started.

Digging a canal across 50 miles (80 km) of wild jungle was an engineering challenge that would take years to complete. An even greater challenge was disease. A French company had begun a canal across Panama more than 20 years earlier, but its efforts ground to a halt, partly because thousands of construction workers died of malaria and yellow fever.

Taft made a personal visit to Panama in late 1904 to assess the situation. To address the problem of tropical disease, he urged the government to give full support to Colonel William C. Gorgas, a medical doctor who earlier helped rid Havana, Cuba, of yellow fever. Gorgas understood that both malaria and yellow fever were transmitted by mosquitoes, and he developed programs to destroy mosquito breeding grounds and protect workers from mosquito bites that might transmit disease. Gorgas's programs drastically reduced the death rates from tropical diseases and contributed to the success of the project.

Taft also had to deal with the resentment of citizens in Panama, who were suspicious of the huge new workforce that arrived to build the canal. They also feared that the United States would take permanent control of their country. Using what one writer called "honeyed words," Taft helped persuade Panamanians that the new canal would become a great benefit to their country.

A third issue involved the critical design and engineering of the canal. In the first few years of construction, two chief engineers had resigned, overwhelmed by the size and difficulty of the project. Taft identified one engineer in Panama who seemed able to master the huge job. He persuaded President

Taft helped manage the huge Panama Canal project, which involved enormous engineering challenges. Above, one of its huge locks under construction. At right, Taft visits the Canal Zone during construction.

Roosevelt to name Major George W. Goethals the chief engineer in 1907. Goethals proved to be the right man for the job. He worked on the canal until it was completed in 1914.

Cuban Peacemaker

The treaty ending the Spanish-American War in 1898 had granted Cuba its independence, but in the years that followed, the United States continued to be involved in Cuban affairs. A constitution for the Cuban government was finally approved by the U.S. Congress in 1901. To the dismay of many Cubans, it included an amendment that gave the United States the right to approve certain Cuban government policies and to intervene in Cuba if U.S. interests there were threatened.

In 1906, Cuban rebels threatened to overthrow the government of Cuban President Tomás Palma. U.S. businessmen with interests in Cuba appealed to the government to protect their property there. Roosevelt and Taft agreed. If a civil war broke out in Cuba, Taft wrote, "some $200,000,000 of American property may go up in smoke in ten days."

Once again, Taft made a personal visit. When he arrived in September 1906, he found the country in a state of anarchy. Palma's government had no support. Government troops controlled only the coast and a few large towns.

Taft soon concluded that the United States should intervene to avoid a destructive war. He ordered almost 8,000 U.S. troops to the island. At the same time, he proclaimed a *provisional* (temporary) government and named himself acting governor.

Taft's decisive actions soon ended the crisis. He ordered the rebels to turn in their weapons, and they quickly obeyed. Ordinary Cubans trusted Taft and seemed relieved that war had been avoided. Two weeks later, Taft appointed American Charles E. Magoon to replace him as provisional governor. The provisional government, backed by U.S. troops, managed Cuban affairs for more than two years. The last troops were withdrawn in January 1909.

Candidate Taft

Taft's successes in Panama and in Cuba received wide publicity, and he became a national figure, widely admired by Americans. It was clear that President Roosevelt trusted his secretary of war and relied on his judgment.

When President Roosevelt ran for election in 1904, he had promised that he would not seek another term. As the 1908 election drew nearer, Taft soon realized that he was one of the favorites to follow Roosevelt to the presidency. The question was whether Taft wanted to be president. Roosevelt urged him to run and promised his support. Nellie had always wanted her husband to be president. His brother Charles also encouraged him to take on the challenge. Still, Taft wasn't sure. He hemmed and hawed, considering the question from every angle.

In the end, Democrat William Jennings Bryan helped Taft make up his mind. Bryan, who was in the running for the Democratic nomination, said in August 1907 that he believed railroads should be taken away from private owners and managed by the government. In Taft's mind, such a step was unthinkable. As a strong supporter of private enterprise, he believed that nationalizing the railroads might bring on a violent revolution. Taft saw it as his duty to keep William Jennings Bryan out of the White House. Bryan's radical suggestion, combined with all the advice Taft received, finally persuaded him. He agreed to run for president.

The Election of 1908 ———————————

When he set his sights on the presidency, William Howard Taft was 50 years old. With the support of President Roosevelt, still the most popular political leader in America, he easily won Republican nomination in June. He resigned his post as secretary of war to concentrate on campaigning. He did not look forward to it, predicting that the campaign would be "kind of a nightmare." It turned out not to be as difficult as he expected. People responded warmly to his candidacy. They liked his sense of humor about himself, and they knew he was honest.

Democrat William Jennings Bryan was Taft's opponent in the 1908 election. Bryan had already run (and lost) twice before, in 1896 and 1900.

Roosevelt himself became impatient with Taft during the campaign. He urged Taft to take stronger stands on issues and to attack Democratic candidate Bryan. Taft appreciated the president's advice, but found it impossible to follow. He was eager to communicate what he stood for, but found it painful to attack another candidate.

Taft did make it clear that he was committed to Roosevelt's principles. He said that his job was to carry out the work started by the current president. This work included prosecuting irresponsible businesses and protecting public lands from private interests. It also included reducing *tariffs* (taxes on goods imported into the country) to encourage world trade and keep consumer prices down at home.

Troublesome Issues

Democrats had difficulty finding ways to attack Taft, who was respected and admired by many voters. One issue they raised was religion. Some attackers pointed out that Taft was a Unitarian, whose church did not support the traditional Christian belief that Jesus was the Son of God. Others took a different tack. Recalling that Taft had negotiated the sale of Roman Catholic lands in the Philippines, they suggested that he was a secret Roman Catholic and would take orders from the pope.

An elaborate souvenir plate from Taft's 1908 campaign (left) shows all the Republican presidential candidates since 1856. Above, Taft gives a campaign speech from the back of his special train during a "whistle-stop" tour.

Taft brushed off the charges, saying, "If the American electorate is so narrow as not to elect a Unitarian, well and good. I can stand it."

By November it was clear that Taft would easily gain election. In November, he received the voting returns at the home of his brother Charles in Cincinnati. He received more than a million more votes than Democrat William Jennings Bryan, and in the electoral college, he received 321 votes to Bryan's 162. The reluctant candidate had been elected president.

Chapter 5

Inauguration ─────────────────

On March 3, 1909, a fierce winter storm slammed into the city of Washington. That night, 70-mile-per-hour (112 km/h) winds lashed the city. Snow fell. By the next morning, inauguration day, the streets and trees of Washington, D.C., were coated with ice. The weather was so miserable that Taft's inauguration ceremonies were moved from the Capitol steps to the Senate Chamber inside. Looking back today, the bad weather seems a fitting symbol of Taft's presidency, which was beset by storms of disagreement.

Taft himself had already shown signs of doubt about succeeding as president. Even before his swearing in, he wrote to a friend, "I look forward to the future with much hesitation and doubt." In his inaugural address that day, he spoke of the "heavy weight of responsibility" he was taking on as president. Once again

On inauguration day, March 4, 1909, a carriage brings outgoing president Roosevelt and incoming president Taft through a blizzard to the Capitol for the ceremony.

he told his audience how proud he was to have served Theodore Roosevelt, and he promised to continue Roosevelt's policies and make his reforms lasting. At the same time, he attempted to calm the fears of business leaders who had felt threatened by Roosevelt's campaign against business monopolies. Taft pledged not to interfere with companies that were pursuing "proper and progressive business methods."

In spite of the chilly inauguration, Taft began his presidency as the people's favorite. Most Americans were convinced that he was able and honest. An editorial in the New York *Sun* said, "Never did any man come to the Presidency before with such universal good will."

Progressives and Conservatives

One of the president's biggest problems was his own party. President Roosevelt had been a pioneer of progressive ideas in the Republican party, and he had managed to keep the party together through the force of his own personality. Now that he was out of office, however, the divisions in the party became clear.

Conservative Republicans had been outraged by Roosevelt's plans to interfere with business by bringing antitrust suits and restricting business use of federal lands. They brought their concerns to Taft and urged him to take a more gentle approach. They also wanted him to support high tariffs, which protected U.S. manufacturers from overseas competition. In their view, one of the roles of the federal government was to protect and encourage private business.

Progressive Republicans, on the other hand, expected Taft to follow Roosevelt's lead. They believed that more antitrust actions should be filed against major corporations. They favored protecting federal lands and lowering tariffs. Taft had promised to carry out Roosevelt's agenda, and progressives in the party wanted to hold him to his promise. They had support from many Democrats, who also favored sterner policies against big business and lower tariffs.

Taft was not well equipped to handle these disputes. He disliked arguments and had difficulty saying no to anyone. He had always disliked the rough-and-tumble of politics, and he found it difficult to take a strong stand for one side or the other. Instead, he kept trying to find compromises that would satisfy both sides. As a former judge, he saw both sides of every issue and weighed them carefully before acting. He was uncomfortable around newspaper reporters and was cautious about what he said. The public rarely learned his "side" of any dispute. He sometimes thought so long and hard about an issue that he delayed action until it was too late.

In short, Taft was not another Roosevelt. Soon those who most admired the former president were becoming suspicious about Taft.

The Taft family poses after his election. Taft's oldest son Robert, upper left, later became an influential Republican senator from Ohio.

Nellie Taft's Illness

The campaign for the presidency and the excitement of moving into the White House proved to be too much for Nellie Taft. In mid-May, she suffered a *stroke* (a ruptured blood vessel in the brain) that left her partially paralyzed and unable to speak. Taft, who had been married to Nellie for almost 25 years, was devastated.

His military aide, Archie Butt, wrote in his diary, "The President looked like a great stricken animal. I have never seen greater suffering or pain . . . on a man's face."

Nellie Taft soon showed her strength. Little by little, over many months, she recovered from the damage the stroke had done. By the end of Taft's term, she was well once again, but during a crucial part of his time in office, Nellie's support and advice had been lost to him. During this time, he was besieged by what he described as a "storm of abuse."

The Tariff Controversy

During the 1908 Republican convention, progressive Republicans made "tariff revision" a plank in the party *platform* (its statement of principles and goals). This was a cause that both Roosevelt and Taft strongly supported, but it was a major change for many Republicans, who had long supported high tariffs to protect U.S. business. Conservative Republicans still favored high tariffs, and they had strong support in Congress.

In 1909, soon after he took office, Taft called a special session of Congress to deal with "revision of the tariff." Conservatives in Congress were ready. Taft's proposal was first taken up by the House of Representatives. There Taft's recommendations were watered down, and the resulting bill lowered tariffs only on a small number of goods. Then the proposal went to the Senate, where conservative Republicans controlled the debate. Led by Senator Nelson W. Aldrich, the Senate rewrote the bill altogether. Most of the tariff reductions disappeared, and tariffs on many items were raised. The Senate leadership claimed that the bill had made tariffs "more fair," even though many had been increased. Through the summer, a committee of the House and Senate members worked toward a compromise. They finally agreed, and the Payne-Aldrich bill was passed by both houses. It did lower tariffs on roughly 650 items. However, it raised tariffs on 220 items and left 1,150 unchanged.

Progressives were shocked at the result. They urged Taft to *veto* the bill (send it back to Congress unsigned) and hold out for real tariff reduction. Yet Taft was reluctant. Senator Aldrich was an old and respected friend who had supported him on other issues. In addition, Taft believed that Congress has the constitutional right to frame and pass laws and that a president should veto a bill only

Senator Nelson Aldrich of Rhode Island led conservative Republicans who revised Taft's tariff bill, keeping most tariffs high.

in emergency situations. Perhaps the biggest reason was that Taft hated open political conflict. Though the bill was not what he had wanted, he signed it into law on August 5, 1909.

Progressive Republicans attacked Taft for signing the bill, breaking the party's promise to lower tariffs. Trying to defend his action, Taft made a major blunder. In a speech, he called Payne-Aldrich "the best tariff bill that the Republican Party has ever passed." He meant that this was the first time Republicans had ever lowered any tariffs, but it sounded as if he supported the bill wholeheartedly. He had lost his first major battle as president. Other battles were already under way.

The Conservation Controversy ——————

As president, Theodore Roosevelt had been the first great conservationist. By executive order, he had protected millions of acres of public land from development. In addition, he had established restrictions on the right of private businesses to carry on logging, mining, and drilling for oil on government lands. He had wide public support for his actions, and people expected Taft to follow Roosevelt's lead. They were to be disappointed.

When Taft took office, many of his cabinet members were holdovers from Roosevelt's presidency. One of these was James Rudolph Garfield, a popular progressive Republican, who was secretary of the interior. His department had responsibility for managing federal lands. In 1909, Taft forced Garfield to resign and appointed Richard Ballinger, a former mayor of Seattle, Washington. Ballinger had many friends in the mining industry and was known to favor licensing government lands for mining and oil drilling. Many conservationists were outraged.

Soon after Ballinger's appointment, Louis Glavis, an employee of the Department of the Interior, accused Ballinger of working to transfer 100,000 acres (40,000 hectares) of public lands in Alaska to a coal-mining company owned by old business associates. Other progressives in the government demanded a full investigation of Ballinger. The most outspoken was Gifford Pinchot, the director of the U.S. Forest Service and a longtime friend of Theodore Roosevelt.

Taft investigated and concluded that Ballinger had done nothing illegal. Soon afterward, Ballinger fired Glavis. Gifford Pinchot kept that dispute alive, however, publicizing the controversy about Ballinger's probusiness views. In early 1910, he wrote a letter to a progressive senator attacking both Ballinger and Taft. When the senator read the letter into the congressional record, Taft was forced to act. Even though Pinchot was the most famous and admired conservationist in the land, Taft fired him for making a direct attack on Ballinger and the president.

Gifford Pinchot was the first director of the U.S. Forest Service and a strong supporter of conservation. He became an outspoken opponent of President Taft, and Taft forced him to resign.

By that time the controversy was spinning out of Taft's control. *Collier's Weekly*, a widely read national magazine, publicized the charges against Ballinger, and soon the public demanded a congressional investigation. Congress eventually concluded that Ballinger had not broken any laws, and the majority report called Ballinger "a competent and honorable gentleman." The investigation had shown, however, that Ballinger did not favor the conservation policies of men like Roosevelt and Gifford Pinchot. Months after the committee released its findings, Ballinger resigned from office and returned to Seattle. The public concluded that Taft, who had appointed Ballinger and defended him, was also not a convinced conservationist.

The Election of 1910

As congressional elections approached in 1910, Taft was being portrayed as a pitiful giant in the White House. According to his opponents, he had lost the tariff battle with Congress, quietly signing a bill he disagreed with. Now it had been shown that he planned to change the government's direction in conservation. His popularity was falling fast with the public and among members of his own party.

The election proved another stunning defeat for the Taft administration. For the first time since 1894, Democrats gained a majority in the U.S. House of Representatives, helped in many cases by the split between progressive and conservative Republicans. Taft understood that with one house of Congress controlled by the opposition, he would have more trouble than ever gaining support for new legislation.

Quiet Successes

Even when it appeared that Taft's presidency was experiencing one public defeat after another, his administration was making quiet progress on a number of issues. Never one to trumpet his own achievements, however, Taft seemed unable to take advantage of his successes.

In the campaign to limit the power of huge corporations, the Taft administration built successfully on the foundation that Theodore Roosevelt had made. Leading companies in many business areas had set up *trusts*, groups of companies in the same industry that were governed by the same directors. A trust could use its power to drive competing companies out of business. When it gained full control of the industry, it could charge high prices and make unlimited profits. The Taft administration followed up on cases already begun and instituted many new suits against "bad" trusts. It oversaw 80 antitrust actions in four years, about twice as many as Roosevelt's administration oversaw in almost eight years.

The largest action was against John D. Rockefeller's Standard Oil Company, the giant company that dominated the nation's oil industry. Standard

Oil's companies produced the oil, refined it, transported it, and sold it to consumers. It had bought out many competing companies and driven others into bankruptcy. Ruling on an antitrust suit pushed by Taft, the Supreme Court ordered that Standard Oil be broken up into seven smaller firms. In making its ruling, the court established a landmark known as the "rule of reason" in antitrust actions. If the government found that a company had used unreasonable and unfair practices to gain an advantage over its competitors, it could order the breakup of the company into smaller units.

Taft also achieved some benefits for working men and women. As president, he oversaw the creation of the Bureau of Mines. One of its responsibilities was to monitor miners' safety and cut down on deaths and injuries. He also

Washington Cherry Blossoms

While Taft struggled through the later years of his presidency, Nellie Taft took action to bring a new kind of beauty to Washington. Remembering the fragrant blossoming cherry trees she had loved in the Philippines, she organized a project to plant thousands of similar trees in the Washington Tidal Basin. The trees still bloom every spring, bringing pleasure to residents and visitors alike. Thanks to Nellie Taft's campaign, the cherry blossoms became a symbol of the nation's capital.

★ ★ ★

Taft supported the antitrust suit against the Standard Oil trust, controlled by John D. Rockefeller. The Supreme Court ruled that the trust should be broken up into smaller companies. Rockefeller remained one of the richest men in America.

established the Children's Bureau to deal with the problem of child labor. To head the bureau he appointed Julia Lathrop, the first woman ever to head a federal government bureau.

In foreign policy matters, Taft was a strong supporter of mediating international disputes, seeking compromises that would reduce the threat of violence or war. He called for submitting many international disputes to *arbitration* (the settlement of a dispute by an impartial judge). He also favored arms-control agreements and the establishment of a multinational peacekeeping navy. These ideas came to nothing when European leaders made it clear they were not interested. European powers were then only a few years from beginning the Great War (now known as World War I).

Early in 1912, Taft had the pleasure of admitting New Mexico and Arizona as the 47th and 48th states of the Union, filling in the outline of the states from coast to coast. The Union would consist of 48 states for nearly 50 years. (Alaska and Hawaii became states in 1959.)

The End of a Beautiful Friendship

Even as Taft struggled with international divisions and a hostile Congress at home, he was faced with a growing challenge in his own party. To his great distress, the challenge was increasingly led by his old friend, Theodore Roosevelt.

The States During the Presidency of William Howard Taft

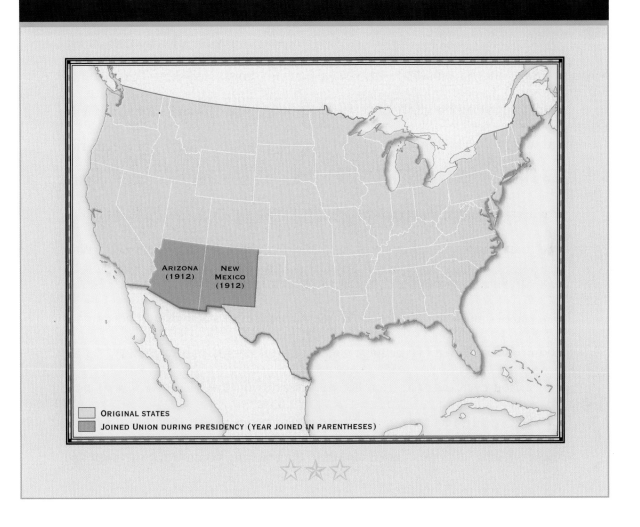

ARIZONA
(1912)

NEW
MEXICO
(1912)

ORIGINAL STATES
JOINED UNION DURING PRESIDENCY (YEAR JOINED IN PARENTHESES)

Soon after Taft's inauguration, Roosevelt had sailed to Africa with a large party to hunt for big game. The former president wanted to avoid any appearance that he was controlling the new president's actions. At the same time, Roosevelt was expecting Taft to continue his programs and follow the direction set during his own years as president. Roosevelt gradually concluded, however, that Taft was changing course. Roosevelt was horrified by the Payne-Aldrich tariff bill, and was angry when Taft appointed Richard Ballinger as secretary of the interior and fired Gifford Pinchot. It was clear to Roosevelt that Taft was betraying the progressive policies of the Roosevelt years.

Taft was torn between two desires. He was eager to keep the former president's friendship and approval. Yet he was determined to prove that he was his own man and not just a stand-in for the former president. He knew he was not another Roosevelt, and he felt that he must conduct the presidency in his own way.

Roosevelt returned from his world travels in June 1910. He was already speaking openly about his opposition to Taft's policies. The friendship between Roosevelt and Taft was strained almost to the breaking point. If the two men had met in person to discuss their differences, they might have been able to mend fences. However, pride on both sides kept them from meeting face to face. Instead, they communicated by letter and through mutual acquaintances. As a result, their disagreements continued to increase.

Theodore Roosevelt returned from a long world tour to became an outspoken critic of President Taft. In this cartoon, "Poppa" Roosevelt addresses a crowd, while Taft, shown as a little boy, thinks, "I wish he'd never come home."

Republican losses in the congressional elections of 1910 increased the strains in the party. Seeing their power slipping away, progressive Republicans looked to Roosevelt. They encouraged him to run for the presidency again in 1912. Roosevelt, still young and vigorous, found the idea attractive. His own political ideas had become even more progressive since he left the presidency, and he came to believe that a change was necessary.

Roosevelt's attacks on Taft became more and more pointed. Taft, always wanting to mend fences rather than openly fight, refused to respond. Finally, late in April 1912, Taft reached the breaking point. He delivered a speech openly attacking Roosevelt's increasingly radical proposals. After the speech, a reporter found the president sitting alone. His head was bowed. "Roosevelt was my closest friend," Taft said. Then he burst into tears.

Roosevelt soon announced that he would be a candidate for the Republican nomination that summer. His supporters entered him into primary elections in several states, in which Republicans could vote for their own preferred candidate. He won nine of the twelve primaries, showing that he had strong support among Republican voters. Primary elections themselves were a new political reform supported by progressives in both parties, and this was the first presidential election in which they played an important role.

During the growing feud with Roosevelt, Taft suffered a tragic loss in his own official family.

Archibald "Archie" Butt had served as White House military aide through the Roosevelt and Taft administrations and had gained the love and respect of both presidents. Early in 1912, Butt had taken a vacation in Europe. In April, he was returning to the United States on the first voyage of the new luxury liner *Titanic*. On April 14, the ship struck an iceberg in the North Atlantic and sank within a few hours. Archie Butt bravely helped women and children into the lifeboats as the ship was sinking. As he said farewell to one young woman friend, he said, "Remember

Taft travels in a carriage with his military assistant, Major Archie Butt. In 1912, Butt died tragically in the sinking of the *Titanic*. He left behind a diary that provided an insider's view of Taft and his presidency.

me to the folks back home." Butt was lost, along with more than 1,500 other passengers and crew. Paying tribute to his friend, President Taft said that Major Butt "died like a soldier and a gentleman."

☆ ☆ ☆

Roosevelt supporters came to the nominating convention in Chicago in June hopeful that their candidate would win the nomination. The convention was a wild affair. As Taft and Roosevelt forces fought for delegates, each side accused the other of bribery and intimidation. The Taft forces controlled the convention process, however. The credentials committee seated delegates who supported Taft and turned away those who supported Roosevelt. When voting began, fights broke out on the floor. Taft's forces won him the nomination, but Roosevelt and his followers charged that he had stolen it.

Roosevelt had threatened that if he was not nominated, he would leave the Republican party and take his supporters with him. After Taft's nomination, Roosevelt made good on his threat. Soon after the Republican convention adjourned, the new Progressive party held its own convention and overwhelmingly nominated Theodore Roosevelt for president.

With three major candidates in the race, the 1912 election divided voters in a way they had never been divided before. Democrat Woodrow Wilson, a member of that party's progressive wing, was elected president. Together, two progressive candidates, Wilson and Roosevelt, won more than two-thirds of the vote, while Taft, the only conservative, won only 23 percent and received the most votes in only two states. It was a decisive defeat for Taft and for conservatives.

Bull Moose Party

When a reporter at the Progressive party's convention asked Roosevelt about his health, he answered with typical confidence. "I'm as fit as a bull moose!" he said. The aggressive bull moose became part of the party's emblem, and it was popularly known as the Bull Moose party.

Roosevelt was nominated by the Bull Moose (or Progressive) party to run against Taft for president in 1912. In this cartoon, every member of the new party looks just like Roosevelt. Both Taft and Roosevelt lost the election to Democrat Woodrow Wilson.

☆ ☆ ☆

It was also a defeat for the Republican party. Taft and Roosevelt together won more than 50 percent of the vote, but they both lost the election. During the campaign, one observer said, "The only question now is which corpse gets the most flowers." Taft was stung by the defeat, the worst ever suffered by a president running for re-election. Still, he was not unhappy to be leaving a job he had hated.

Chapter 6

Professor Taft ———————————————

William Howard Taft was relieved to leave the presidency. After Woodrow Wilson's election in November, he began to relax, even though he had four months left to serve. His sense of humor returned. "The nearer I get to the inauguration of my successor," he said in a letter to a friend, "the greater the relief I feel."

At first, Taft thought he would practice law in Cincinnati when he left the presidency. Then he received an offer to become a professor at the law school of Yale University. This seemed a perfect fit. The job would offer him a chance to return to the scenes of his own college days and to teach the subject he loved best of all—the law. In addition, residence in New Haven, Connecticut, would keep the Tafts near their children. Robert was studying at the Harvard Law School in Massachusetts. Helen was a student at Bryn Mawr College

The Taft Family

Young Robert Taft would return to Ohio after his studies at Harvard and carry on the Taft tradition of political leadership and public service. He was elected to the Ohio state legislature and later to the U.S. Senate, where he served from 1939 to 1953. Known as "Mr. Republican" to his followers, he sought the Republican nomination for president in 1940, 1948, and 1952, but lost each time.

Robert Taft's son, Robert A. Taft Jr., represented Ohio in the U.S. House of Representatives for three terms, then in the U.S. Senate from 1971 until 1977. His son, Robert A. Taft II, known as Bob, was elected governor of Ohio in 1998 and re-elected in 2002. Bob Taft is the fifth generation of his remarkable family to serve in high state or federal office.

in Pennsylvania. Charles, the youngest, was even closer. He was studying at the Taft School in Watertown, Connecticut. The school's headmaster was the former president's brother, Horace Taft.

The next eight years were happy ones for Taft. He enjoyed teaching, and he had time for many other pursuits. He became a popular public speaker and wrote extensively for publication. He and Nellie were able to entertain friends and to travel during school breaks. He also kept up his interest in politics. He never showed a desire to run for elective office, but he was willing to contribute his knowledge and skills to the government. In 1913 and 1914, he served as president of the Lincoln Memorial Commission. This group was in charge of the construction of the memorial that now graces the National Mall in Washington, D.C.

In 1914, war (now known as World War I) broke out in Europe. Like many Americans, Taft hoped that the war would not draw the United States into battle and was dedicated to the idea that it was possible to avoid war. In 1915, he became president of the League to Enforce Peace. This organization believed that international conflicts could be resolved without war, by submitting disagreements to an international court. Members of the league also promised to act together against any member nation that committed hostile acts against another.

By 1917, circumstances had changed, and Congress declared war on Germany and the other Central Powers. Taft threw his support behind the war effort. He promoted the sale of Liberty Bonds (government bonds sold to finance the war effort). He also served as joint chairman of the War Labor Board, a group of influential men appointed by President Wilson to serve as a court of last resort in wartime labor disputes.

At the end of the war, President Wilson proposed that the peace agreement include organization of the League of Nations. Taft wholeheartedly supported Wilson's proposal and urged fellow Republicans to back it. In this case, Taft was out of step with fellow conservative Republicans. They were deeply

Taft as a law professor at Yale University after he left the White House. He is dressed in academic robes.

opposed to the League of Nations. In fact, Taft's old friend Henry Cabot Lodge led the opposition to the league in the U.S. Senate, and the United States never did join the international organization.

In 1919, as the battle over the League of Nations raged, Theodore Roosevelt died. Taft and Roosevelt had met one last time in 1918, about six months before Roosevelt's death. They were cordial to each other, but they were never able to rekindle their old friendship. Still, Taft was grateful for the meeting. "Had he died in a hostile state of mind to me," Taft said, "I would have mourned the fact all my life. I loved him always and cherish his memory."

A Dream Comes True

In 1920, the Republicans nominated and elected Warren Harding as president. By this time, the party was firmly in the hands of conservatives, and Harding had won election by opposing U.S. membership in the League of Nations. He pledged a "return to normalcy"—harking back to the way things were before the United States got involved in international affairs and wars.

After his inauguration in 1921, President Harding promised Taft he would be appointed to the Supreme Court as soon as there was an opening. Soon afterward, Chief Justice Edward White died, and on June 30 Harding appointed Taft as chief justice. The appointment was confirmed by the Senate the same day.

President Warren Harding

Warren Harding was the publisher of a daily newspaper in Marion, Ohio, and had been active in Republican politics for decades. He first came to national notice at the Republican convention in 1912, when he delivered the nominating speech for William Howard Taft.

Harding was elected to the U.S. Senate in 1914, and in 1920 he was elected president. He died in office in August 1923.

☆ ★ ☆

For Taft, the appointment to the Supreme Court was the fulfillment of a dream, and he came to see it as a kind of repayment for the misery he had experienced as president. A few years later, he wrote, "The truth is that in my present life I don't remember that I ever was president."

Happy as he was, Taft found service on the court to be hard work. There was a huge backlog of cases awaiting the court's decision. More than 340 cases were awaiting argument when he was sworn in, and another 421 were filed during the next ten months. No longer a young man (he was 63 when appointed), he pushed himself and his fellow justices hard to clear the heavy caseload. He rose every day at 5:15 a.m. and worked late in the evening. He soon realized, though, that other steps would have to be taken.

Taft (seated at center) finally realized his lifetime ambition in 1921, when he was appointed Chief Justice of the United States. He is shown here with the full Supreme Court in 1930, shortly before his retirement.

Taft concluded that changes were needed to keep the court from being snowed under by cases. When he began, the court was required to hear any appeal from a lower federal court in which either side claimed the Constitution was involved. Taft urged Congress to give the court more control over its workload. Finally, in 1924, new legislation allowed the court to hear only cases it thought worthy of consideration.

Taft also urged the government to plan a permanent home for the Supreme Court. From the nation's earliest days, the court had met in a variety of locations, never in a place they could call their own. In 1929 Congress authorized the construction of a new Supreme Court Building near the U.S. Capitol.

Respected Jurist

Taft wrote many court decisions during his tenure, but he was not known primarily for his deep legal reasoning or devotion to a particular cause. His larger contribution may have been mediating between other strong-minded justices to produce strong legal decisions. Among the most famous (and opinionated) associate judges were Louis Brandeis, a former adviser to Democratic president Woodrow Wilson, and Oliver Wendell Holmes Jr., a legendary judge who had fought in the Civil War and had served on the court since 1902.

Taft believed that for a judge, the law takes precedence over personal beliefs. He personally did not favor the constitutional amendment prohibiting sale of alcoholic beverages. When a bill to enforce the amendment was challenged, however, Taft voted to uphold it. In another decision, Taft ruled that the meat-packing industry could be regulated by the federal government. Investigative reporters had revealed that the industry often sold rotting or diseased meat and that it subjected its employees to dangerous working conditions. Taft also ruled that a federal income tax amendment was constitutional.

Once he took on the responsibilities as chief justice, Taft began to lose weight, likely a sign that the job was satisfying to him. Soon he weighed less than 250 pounds (113 kg). Still, Taft's weight had taken a toll on his health. By 1923, the year he celebrated his 66th birthday, his heart was beginning to fail. He was forced to cut down his work schedule and to limit his activities outside the court.

At the end of 1929, Taft's half brother Charles died in Cincinnati. Charles had been an important supporter and adviser to Taft throughout his adult life. He insisted on attending the funeral even though he was ill himself. When he returned to Washington, he was exhausted, and his doctor ordered him to rest. His condition worsened, however, and on February 3, 1930, he resigned as chief justice. Just a few weeks later, on March 8, he died. He was 72 years old.

Legacy

Most historians consider Taft's term as president a failure. He had the misfortune of following Theodore Roosevelt, one of the most dynamic and popular presidents in history, and he could not live up to Roosevelt's performance. Taft soon discovered that his dislike of political maneuvering and his hatred of open conflict were serious handicaps in succeeding as president. He seemed unable to build a coalition of supporters in Congress and in the country, and he was often reluctant to advertise his own successes. He had a tendency to try to make everybody happy, often succeeding in making no one happy.

Taft had great talents as an administrator, however. These were displayed in the Philippines, where he helped organize a government and gain the trust of a recently conquered people. In supervising work on the Panama Canal, he contributed to the completion of a huge project by dealing not only with the engineering but with the health of the workforce and the fears of the Panamanian people. As president, he successfully pressed antitrust cases against a wide range of business giants, and he supported new government offices to look out for the health and safety of workers.

In the end, Taft's cautious nature helped to ally him with conservative leaders at a time when the country was demanding further progressive reforms.

President William Howard Taft.

Taft's gravestone at Arlington National Cemetery, in Virginia near Washington, D.C.

The failure of Taft and Roosevelt to come to some agreement in 1912 was the major tragedy in Taft's long career. It resulted in the most devastating defeat ever suffered by a president running for reelection. In the end, the defeat may have saved Taft by rescuing him from the presidency and allowing him to serve years later as chief justice.

As chief justice, Taft helped streamline court procedures and helped persuade the government to build a permanent home for the court. He also presided over a court that upheld the constitutionality of new progressive legislation.

Taft is remembered neither as a great president nor as a great chief justice. The fact remains, however, that he is the only person in U.S. history who ever served in both positions. In his long career, friends and foes alike acknowledged his great talents, his honesty, and his devotion to public service.

Fast Facts William Howard Taft

Birth:	September 15, 1857
Birthplace:	Cincinnati, Ohio
Parents:	Alphonso Taft and Louisa Maria Torrey Taft
Brothers & Sisters:	Charles (1843–1929) (half brother)
	Peter (1845–1889) (half brother)
	Henry (1859–1945)
	Horace (1861–1943)
	Frances (Fanny) (1865–1950)
Education:	Yale University, graduated 1878
	Cincinnati Law School, 1878–1880
Occupation:	Lawyer, judge
Marriage:	To Helen Herron, June 19, 1886
Children:	(see First Lady Fast Facts at right)
Political Party:	Republican
Public Offices:	1881 Assistant Prosecuting Attorney, Hamilton County, Ohio
	1882–1883 Collector of Internal Revenue, Cincinnati District
	1887–1890 Ohio Superior Court Judge
	1890–1892 U.S. Solicitor General
	1892–1900 Federal Circuit Court Judge
	1900–1901 President of the Philippine Commission
	1901–1904 Civil Governor of the Philippines
	1904–1908 Secretary of War
	1909–1912 27th President of the United States
	1921–1930 Chief Justice of the United States
His Vice President:	James S. Sherman (died in office October 30, 1912)
Major Actions as President:	1909 Fought for reduced tariff rates
	1910 Supported Richard Ballinger in conservation controversy
	1911 Urged new tariff treaty with Canada
Death:	Washington, D.C., March 8, 1930
Age at Death:	72 years
Burial Place:	Arlington National Cemetery, Arlington, Virginia

Fast Facts Helen Herron (Nellie) Taft

Birth:	June 2, 1861
Birthplace:	Cincinnati, Ohio
Parents:	John Herron and Harriet Collens Herron
Sisters & Brothers	One of 11 children
Education:	Miss Nourse's School, Cincinnati
	Miami University, Oxford, Ohio
	University of Cincinnati (music)
Marriage:	To William Howard Taft, June 19, 1886
Children:	Robert Alphonso (1889–1953)
	Helen (1891–1987)
	Charles (1897–1983)
Firsts:	Pushed for planting of Japanese cherry trees around the Tidal Basin in Washington, D.C.
Death:	May 22, 1943
Age at Death:	Nearly 82 years
Burial Place:	Arlington National Cemetery, Arlington, Virginia

Timeline

1857	1870	1874	1878	1881
William Howard Taft born in Cincinnati, Ohio, September 15	Enters Woodward High School, Cincinnati	Enters Yale University	Graduates from Yale; begins law study at Cincinnati Law School	Becomes assistant prosecutor of Hamilton County, Ohio

1891	1892	1897	1900	1901
Daughter Helen born	Appointed judge of U.S. Circuit Court of Appeals	Son Charles born	Becomes president of the Philippine Commission	Appointed civil governor of the Philippines

1910	1911	1912	1913	1918
Supports Richard Ballinger in conservation controversy	Fires conservationist Gifford Pinchot	Breaks with Roosevelt, loses three-way presidential election to Woodrow Wilson	Appointed a professor of law at Yale University law school	Appointed joint chairman of National War Labor Board

1882	1886	1887	1889	1890
Appointed district collector of internal revenue	Marries Helen (Nellie) Herron	Appointed judge on the Ohio Superior Court	Son Robert A. Taft born	Named Solicitor General of the United States

1902	1904	1906	1908	1909
Negotiates with Pope Leo XIII over church lands in the Philippines	Appointed secretary of war in cabinet of President Theodore Roosevelt	Intervenes in Cuba to end revolution	Elected president	Fights for tariff reductions

1921	1930
Appointed Chief Justice of the United States	Taft resigns as chief justice, February; dies March 8

Glossary

arbitration: the settlement of a dispute by an impartial judge or court

bar examination: the test taken by law students to obtain a license to practice law

cede: to grant or surrender territory by treaty

clairvoyant powers: the ability to see things unseen by other people

injunction: a legal order prohibiting a certain action

insurrection: an uprising or revolution against established authority

platform: a statement of a political party's principles and goals

provisional: temporary, pending a permanent arrangement or appointment

strike: a refusal to work until certain demands are met

stroke: a ruptured blood vessel in the brain

tariffs: duties or taxes on imported goods

trusts: groups of businesses organized to defeat competition or increase prices

typhoon: a tropical storm in the Eastern Hemisphere, similar to a hurricane

veto: in U.S. government, the refusal of the president to sign a bill passed by Congress into law

Further Reading

Joseph, Paul. *William Taft.* Edina, MN: Abdo Publishing, 2001.

Maupin, Melissa. *William Howard Taft: Our 27th President.* Chanhassen, MN: Child's World, 2002.

O'Connell, Kim A. *William Howard Taft.* Berkeley Heights, NJ: MyReportLinks.com Books, 2003.

MORE ADVANCED READING

Manners, William. *TR and Will: A Friendship That Split the Republican Party.* New York: Harcourt Brace & World, 1969.

Pringle, Henry F. *The Life and Times of William Howard Taft,* 2 volumes. New York: Farrar & Rinehart, 1939.

Taft, Helen Herron. *Recollections of Full Years.* New York: Dodd, Mead & Company, 1914.

Places to Visit

★ ★ ★ ★ ★

William Howard Taft National Historic Site

2038 Auburn Avenue
Cincinnati, OH 45219
(513) 684-3262
www.nps.gov/wiho/index.htm

This is the house where Taft was born. Restored to its original appearance, the house is now a museum with exhibits about Taft, his family, and life.

Grave of William Howard Taft

Arlington National Cemetery
Arlington, VA

Taft was the first president to be interred in this national military cemetery across the Potomac River from Washington, D.C. His wife, Helen Herron Taft, was later buried next to him. John F. Kennedy and Jacqueline Kennedy Onassis are the only other president and first lady buried in Arlington National Cemetery.

The White House

1600 Pennsylvania Avenue NW
Washington, DC 20500
24-hour Visitors' Office Info Line:
(202) 456-7041

William Howard and Helen Taft lived here from 1909 to 1913.

Online Sites of Interest

★ **Internet Public Library, Presidents of the United States (IPL–POTUS)**

http:// www.ipl.org/div/potus/whtaft.html

Includes concise information about Taft and his presidency and provides links to other sites of interest.

★ **American President.org**

http://www.americanpresident.org/history/

Offers an informative biography of Taft, including background information on his early life, family, career, and presidency. This site provides biographies of all the presidents.

★ **Scholastic/Grolier**

http://ap.grolier.com

This site, sponsored by a publisher of reference material, offers materials for every president at different reading levels.

★ **Taft's Sense of Humor**

www.stretching-it.com/taft/taft_humor_pg1.htm

This author-sponsored site features the lighter side of Taft, illustrating his own sense of humor and recounting amusing stories about him.

★ **The White House**

www.whitehouse.gov/history/presidents

Offers brief biographical articles on each president and first lady.

★ **William Howard Taft National Historic Site**

www.nps.gov/wiho/index.htm

This site provides a view of the house in which Taft was born. It also provides information about his life and presidency.

★ **Arlington National Cemetery**

www.arlingtoncemetery.net/whtaft.htm

Offers photos of Taft's burial place, a brief biography, and a lengthy article printed in the *New York Times* on March 9, 1930, the day after Taft's death.

Table of Presidents

	1. George Washington	**2. John Adams**	**3. Thomas Jefferson**	**4. James Madison**
Took office	Apr 30 1789	Mar 4 1797	Mar 4 1801	Mar 4 1809
Left office	Mar 3 1797	Mar 3 1801	Mar 3 1809	Mar 3 1817
Birthplace	Westmoreland Co, VA	Braintree, MA	Shadwell, VA	Port Conway, VA
Birth date	Feb 22 1732	Oct 20 1735	Apr 13 1743	Mar 16 1751
Death date	Dec 14 1799	July 4 1826	July 4 1826	June 28 1836

   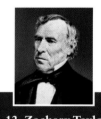

	9. William H. Harrison	**10. John Tyler**	**11. James K. Polk**	**12. Zachary Taylor**
Took office	Mar 4 1841	Apr 6 1841	Mar 4 1845	Mar 5 1849
Left office	**Apr 4 1841•**	Mar 3 1845	Mar 3 1849	**July 9 1850•**
Birthplace	Berkeley, VA	Greenway, VA	Mecklenburg Co, NC	Barboursville, VA
Birth date	Feb 9 1773	Mar 29 1790	Nov 2 1795	Nov 24 1784
Death date	Apr 4 1841	Jan 18 1862	June 15 1849	July 9 1850

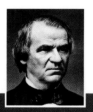   

	17. Andrew Johnson	**18. Ulysses S. Grant**	**19. Rutherford B. Hayes**	**20. James A. Garfield**
Took office	Apr 15 1865	Mar 4 1869	Mar 5 1877	Mar 4 1881
Left office	Mar 3 1869	Mar 3 1877	Mar 3 1881	**Sept 19 1881•**
Birthplace	Raleigh, NC	Point Pleasant, OH	Delaware, OH	Orange, OH
Birth date	Dec 29 1808	Apr 27 1822	Oct 4 1822	Nov 19 1831
Death date	July 31 1875	July 23 1885	Jan 17 1893	Sept 19 1881

5. James Monroe	6. John Quincy Adams	7. Andrew Jackson	8. Martin Van Buren
Mar 4 1817	Mar 4 1825	Mar 4 1829	Mar 4 1837
Mar 3 1825	Mar 3 1829	Mar 3 1837	Mar 3 1841
Westmoreland Co, VA	Braintree, MA	The Waxhaws, SC	Kinderhook, NY
Apr 28 1758	July 11 1767	Mar 15 1767	Dec 5 1782
July 4 1831	Feb 23 1848	June 8 1845	July 24 1862

13. Millard Fillmore	14. Franklin Pierce	15. James Buchanan	16. Abraham Lincoln
July 9 1850	Mar 4 1853	Mar 4 1857	Mar 4 1861
Mar 3 1853	Mar 3 1857	Mar 3 1861	**Apr 15 1865•**
Locke Township, NY	Hillsborough, NH	Cove Gap, PA	Hardin Co, KY
Jan 7 1800	Nov 23 1804	Apr 23 1791	Feb 12 1809
Mar 8 1874	Oct 8 1869	June 1 1868	Apr 15 1865

21. Chester A. Arthur	22. Grover Cleveland	23. Benjamin Harrison	24. Grover Cleveland
Sept 19 1881	Mar 4 1885	Mar 4 1889	Mar 4 1893
Mar 3 1885	Mar 3 1889	Mar 3 1893	Mar 3 1897
Fairfield, VT	Caldwell, NJ	North Bend, OH	Caldwell, NJ
Oct 5 1829	Mar 18 1837	Aug 20 1833	Mar 18 1837
Nov 18 1886	June 24 1908	Mar 13 1901	June 24 1908

	25. William McKinley	**26. Theodore Roosevelt**	**27. William H. Taft**	**28. Woodrow Wilson**
Took office	Mar 4 1897	Sept 14 1901	Mar 4 1909	Mar 4 1913
Left office	**Sept 14 1901•**	Mar 3 1909	Mar 3 1913	Mar 3 1921
Birthplace	Niles, OH	New York, NY	Cincinnati, OH	Staunton, VA
Birth date	Jan 29 1843	Oct 27 1858	Sept 15 1857	Dec 28 1856
Death date	Sept 14 1901	Jan 6 1919	Mar 8 1930	Feb 3 1924

	33. Harry S. Truman	**34. Dwight D. Eisenhower**	**35. John F. Kennedy**	**36. Lyndon B. Johnson**
Took office	Apr 12 1945	Jan 20 1953	Jan 20 1961	Nov 22 1963
Left office	Jan 20 1953	Jan 20 1961	**Nov 22 1963•**	Jan 20 1969
Birthplace	Lamar, MO	Denison, TX	Brookline, MA	Johnson City, TX
Birth date	May 8 1884	Oct 14 1890	May 29 1917	Aug 27 1908
Death date	Dec 26 1972	Mar 28 1969	Nov 22 1963	Jan 22 1973

	41. George Bush	**42. Bill Clinton**	**43. George W. Bush**	
Took office	Jan 20 1989	Jan 20 1993	Jan 20 2001	
Left office	Jan 20 1993	Jan 20 2001	—	
Birthplace	Milton, MA	Hope, AR	New Haven, CT	
Birth date	June 12 1924	Aug 19 1946	July 6 1946	
Death date	—	—	—	

29. Warren G. Harding	**30. Calvin Coolidge**	**31. Herbert Hoover**	**32. Franklin D. Roosevelt**
Mar 4 1921	Aug 2 1923	Mar 4 1929	Mar 4 1933
Aug 2 1923•	Mar 3 1929	Mar 3 1933	**Apr 12 1945•**
Blooming Grove, OH	Plymouth, VT	West Branch, IA	Hyde Park, NY
Nov 21 1865	July 4 1872	Aug 10 1874	Jan 30 1882
Aug 2 1923	Jan 5 1933	Oct 20 1964	Apr 12 1945

37. Richard M. Nixon	**38. Gerald R. Ford**	**39. Jimmy Carter**	**40. Ronald Reagan**
Jan 20 1969	Aug 9 1974	Jan 20 1977	Jan 20 1981
Aug 9 1974★	Jan 20 1977	Jan 20 1981	Jan 20 1989
Yorba Linda, CA	Omaha, NE	Plains, GA	Tampico, IL
Jan 9 1913	July 14 1913	Oct 1 1924	Feb 6 1911
Apr 22 1994	—	—	June 5 2004

• Indicates the president died while in office.

★ Richard Nixon resigned before his term expired.

Index

About the Author

Kieran Doherty is the award-winning author of 13 books for young readers. A career journalist and magazine writer before turning his attention to writing for children and teens, he particularly enjoys writing historical nonfiction. Doherty, an avid sailor, lives in Lake Worth, Florida, with his wife, Lynne.